DETROIT PUBLIC LIBRARY

3 5674 01641226 5

j
F45g

W9-BWR-922

Eugene Field

The Gingham Dog and the Calico Cat

· Illustrated by Janet Street ·

Philomel Books · New York

JE

The Gingham Dog and the Calico Cat contains the text of
Eugene Field's poem ''The Duel'' in its entirety.

Copyright © 1990 by Janet Street. All rights reserved.
Published by Philomel Books, a division of The Putnam & Grosset Group,
200 Madison Avenue, New York, NY 10016. Published simultaneously in Canada.
First Sandcastle Books Edition published in 1993.
Sandcastle Books and the Sandcastle logo are trademarks
belonging to The Putnam & Grosset Group. Printed in Hong Kong.
Book design by Golda Laurens.

Library of Congress Cataloging-in-Publication Data.
Field, Eugene, 1850-1895. The gingham dog and the calico cat/by Eugene Field;
illustrated by Janet Street. p. cm.
Summary: A fight erupts during the middle of the night
between two stuffed animals in an antique shop.
1. Toys—Juvenile poetry.   2. Children's poetry. American.
[1. Toys—Poetry.   2. Dogs—Poetry.   3. Cats—Poetry.   4. American
poetry.]   I. Street, Janet, ill.   II. Title.
PS1667.G56   1990   811'.4—dc20   89-70961   CIP   AC
ISBN 0-399-22151-4 (hardcover)
3   5   7   9   10   8   6   4
ISBN 0-399-22517-X (Sandcastle)
1   3   5   7   9   10   8   6   4   2
First Sandcastle Books Edition

KN   JUL '93

To my family,
Virginia, Ed, Gordon, and Hunt.
And special thanks to Jane Yolen.
J.S.

The gingham dog and the calico cat
Side by side on the table sat;

'Twas half-past twelve, and (what do you think!)
Nor one nor t'other had slept a wink!

The old Dutch clock and the Chinese plate
Appeared to know as sure as fate

There was going to be a terrible spat.

(I wasn't there; I simply state
What was told to me by the Chinese plate!)

The gingham dog went "bow-wow-wow!"

And the calico cat replied "mee-ow!"

The air was littered, an hour or so,
With bits of gingham and calico,

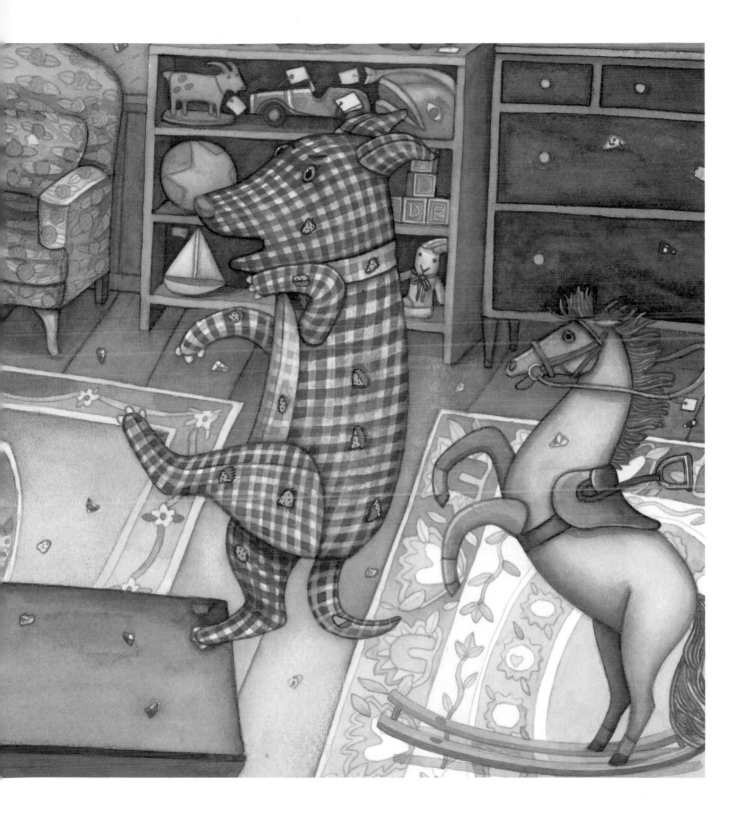

While the old Dutch clock in the chimney-place
Up with its hands before its face,

For it always dreaded a family row!

*(Now mind; I'm only telling you
What the old Dutch clock declares is true!)*

The Chinese plate looked very blue,
And wailed, "Oh dear! what shall we do!"

But the gingham dog and the calico cat
Wallowed this way and tumbled that,

Employing every tooth and claw
In the awfullest way you ever saw—
And, oh! how the gingham and calico flew!

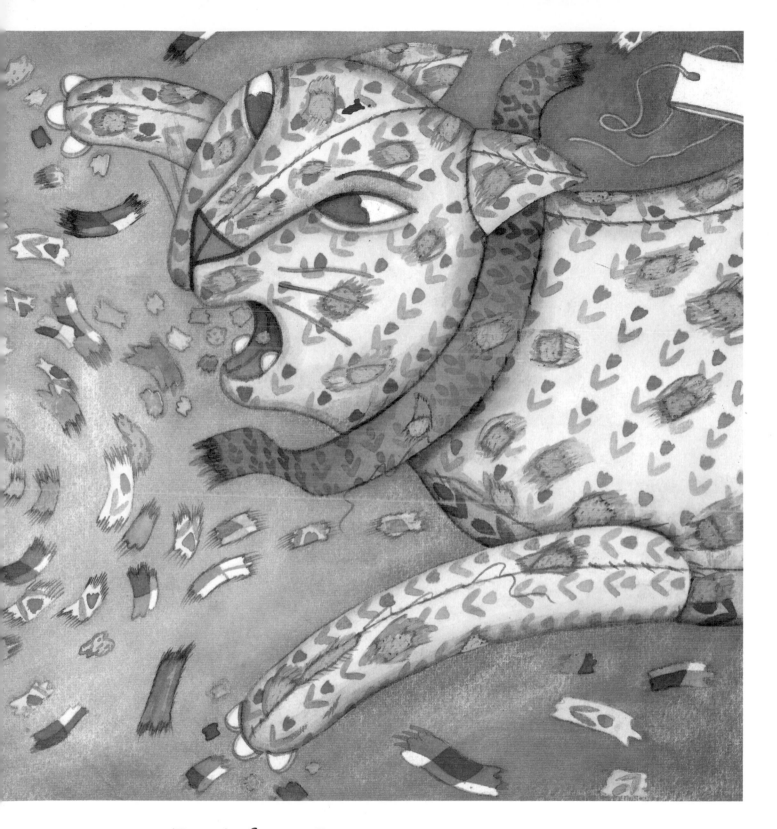

(Don't fancy I exaggerate—
I got my news from the Chinese plate!)

Next morning, where the two had sat
They found no trace of dog or cat;

And some folks think unto this day
That burglars stole that pair away!

But the truth about the cat and pup
Is this: they ate each other up!

Now what do you really think of that!

(The old Dutch clock it told me so,
And that is how I came to know.)